636 ISE

D0518056

(2nd copy)
$13.31
Fawett D.O. 20902   8

BABY ANIMALS
ON THE FARM

BABY ANIMALS
ON THE FARM

by **Hans-Heinrich Isenbart**

photographs by **Ruth Rau**

translated by
Elizabeth D. Crawford

G. P. Putnam's Sons   New York

Copyright © 1981 by Kinderbuchverlag Reich, Luzern AG.
First published in Switzerland.
Photos on pages 10 (above) and 27 by Jacana (Veiller & Varin—Visage);
on page 26 by Othmar Baumli; and on page 35 by Bio-Info.
All rights reserved. Published simultaneously in Canada.
Book design by Virginia Evans.
Printed in Hong Kong by South China Printing Co. (1988) Ltd.
Library of Congress Cataloging in Publication Data
Isenbart, Hans-Heinrich
Baby animals on the farm.
Translation of: Ferkel, Fohlen, Kitz und Co.
Summary: Text and photographs present
farm animals in their infancy.
1. Domestic animals—Infancy—Juvenile literature.
2. Animals—Infancy—Juvenile literature.
[1. Domestic animals—Infancy. 2. Animals—Infancy]
I. Rau, Ruth, ill. II. Crawford, Elizabeth D. III. Title.
SF75.5.I8313 1984   636'.07   84-6947
ISBN 0-399-61225-4
5   7   9   10   8   6

BABY ANIMALS
ON THE FARM

Most of the animals you will find in this book are representative of animals raised on farms all over the world. They fall into two categories: precocial and altricial.

Precocial animals come into the world so well-developed that they can get about on their own as soon as they are born. Their eyes are open so that they can look for their own food. They have fur or down—the soft underfeathers of birds—to protect them from the cold. Of the mammals, horses, donkeys, cows, pigs, goats and sheep are precocial animals. So are the birds: the chickens, ducks, geese, swans and turkeys.

Altricial animals are not so strong and developed at birth that they can live without the warmth and care of their mother. They are born in an immature and helpless state. Their eyes are closed for about ten days and they cannot move by themselves. Of the mammals, dogs, cats and rabbits are altricial animals; so are the pigeons.

This young colt is enjoying a sunny day in the meadow with his mother, a mare. He likes to run after her, kicking up his heels. He is still young and exercise helps him to grow bigger and stronger. It will be some time before he wears a saddle and bridle, but one day the children on the farm will ride him.

D onkeys can be found on farms all over the world. Although they are related to the horse, they are usually smaller. Donkeys are good-natured, hard workers, and it is not true that they are stubborn. They will patiently carry heavy loads over long distances, their foals trotting along beside them.

Foals are playful and alert and fun to play with on the farm. They aren't put to work until they have grown up and are sturdy and strong.

This little colt is learning to stand and walk. When he gets tired from trying, he rests until his mother nudges him gently to stand up and try again.

These calves have been born outside in the fields because the weather is warm. If it had been cold, they would have been born in the barn. Like horse and donkey foals, calves can stand by themselves soon after they are born. But they stay close to their mothers, resting and eating.

This lucky calf is getting its milk from its mother. On many farms, calves are separated from their mothers and fed by the farmer, so that he can measure exactly how much milk the calf drinks.

This mother pig is lying in clean straw, feeding her nine little piglets. When the piglets are not eating or sleeping, they are very energetic. They rush around the pen, shoving and thumping each other playfully, grunting and squeaking excitedly.

Their pen is clean and warm. Pigs are not dirty animals, even

though they sometimes wallow in mud in the farmyard. Actually, pigs roll in mud to cool off and get clean. The pig covers itself in mud, and as the mud dries, fleas and lice are trapped. Then it scratches the mud off on a tree trunk or fence, leaving itself clean and free of insects.

The goat is an important animal on farms in many places where people depend on goats for milk and cheese. The goat is a hardy animal and can manage to find something to eat even in hot countries where there is little grass for grazing and not much rain.

Baby goats are called kids. They have baby voices that sound almost whiney when they call their mothers—*m-a-a-a-a*.

B aby lambs are born on the farm in the spring. Usually around April, one can see them prancing and leaping together in the fields. They make a long, drawn-out *b-a-a-a-a* sound.

These sheep provide the farm with wool. Twice a year, the

shepherd shears them, and their thick fur, called fleece, is spun into wool for clothing such as sweaters, gloves, scarves and warm socks.

If there is a large herd of sheep on the farm, the shepherd cares for them with the help of a sheep dog.

ried eggs, scrambled eggs, omelets and Easter eggs! We wouldn't have any of these without our hens. When the hen lays an egg, she announces the event with a loud cackle.

Most of the hen's eggs are gathered from her nest for eating. But if a rooster lives with the hen and fertilizes her eggs, tiny, fluffy chicks can be born.

S carcely an hour after they have hatched from their eggs, furry little ducklings are standing on their webbed feet ready for a swim. If the mother leads them to water on the day they are born, they will hop right in.

The chicks peep with clear little voices. The father, a drake, gives out a soft *raaayb, raaayb*. The mother duck, especially in winter when she is calling a drake, makes a loud *naaaattt, naaaattt* sound.

G eese are large, heavy birds which make loud, piercing, trumpeting sounds, especially when a stranger enters the farmyard.

From ducks and geese, we get soft, fluffy feathers, called down, which is used to fill pillows, comforters and jackets. These things keep us very warm in cold weather.

This mother swan with the black knob over her bill is called a mute swan because she makes almost no sound. When her baby swans are born, they have a light, downy coat that changes to gray brown after a few months. They will not become pure white until they are four years old.

The father swan takes good care of his family. He keeps watch around the nest and he takes his turn sitting on the eggs. Both the mother and father swan share everything they find to eat with their young.

When settlers from Europe arrived in this country, they found birds in the forests that they had never seen before—wild turkeys. Turkeys seldom fly, even in the wild. They prefer to walk on their sturdy, strong legs like this ten-day-old chick. The mother turkey opposite has some other baby chicks visiting besides her own light-colored babies.

Unlike animals such as foals and fluffy chicks, these little puppies were born with their eyes closed and completely dependent on their mother for food and care. Now they are ten days old, and their eyes are open, but they still must be kept warm, cleaned and fed by their mother. They are most content when they can snuggle up for some milk.

This little kitten is just being born. Like puppies, its eyes are closed at birth and will stay closed for about ten days. But it won't be long before the kitten will be lively and playful like the kittens on the opposite page, who like to stalk and pounce on one another. This kind of play is good practice for hunting mice in the barn when the kittens are fully grown.

The tiny rabbit below is sitting close to its mother, where it feels warm and safe. Even so, its ears are alert and listening. When it was born, it didn't have a furry coat, and its eyes were tightly closed. Now it is living and growing in a hutch on the farm, unlike its wild cousins, which live in burrows (called "warrens") underground.

Here a mother pigeon is feeding her chick in the nest. Both the mother and father pigeon take turns sitting on the eggs before the baby is hatched. Usually there are two little chicks born after seventeen days inside their eggs.

Pigeons in the nest make a gentle cooing sound: *coo-coo-coo*.

Notes on the Animals

Precocial

HORSE

Male: stallion. Castrated (that is, made sterile so that he cannot sire any more young): gelding
Female: mare
Young: foal, colt (male), filly (female)

After a gestation period of eleven months, the mare bears one foal (or, rarely, two), which can stand up on its long legs and follow its mother about an hour after birth. When horses and donkeys have babies, the process is called "foaling," from the name for the young. For working in the field or for pulling heavy burdens, people used to use the heavy, quiet horses called workhorses. Today you usually see saddle horses or ponies in the fields, as horses are mostly used for riding. Thoroughbred horses are seen in riding stables and at the racetrack.

DONKEY

Male: stallion (sometimes called jack)
Female: mare (sometimes called jenny)
Young: foal, colt (male), filly (female)

After a gestation period of thirteen months, the mare gives birth to one foal. Donkeys are plant-eaters ("herbivores") and are more placid and patient than horses. Donkeys have long ears, a tasseled tail, and a voice that cannot be ignored. If a horse mare and a donkey stallion mate, their offspring are "mules." If a donkey mare and a horse stallion mate, "hinnies" are the result.

COW

Male: bull. Castrated: steer, ox
Female: cow; heifer (that is, a cow that has yet to "calve"—bear a calf—for the first time)
Young: calf

You can tell by her horns how many calves the cow has had already because with each birth a new ring of horn grows. After a gestation period of forty weeks, one or two calves are born and are immediately independent. The cow is a grazing animal, a plant-eater, but unlike the donkey and the horse, it is a "ruminant." The cow grazes until the "rumen," or first stomach, is filled. There the food is superdigested and then sent to a second stomach called the "reticulum," where it is made into little balls of "cud." Now the cow brings the cud back into her mouth, chews the food a second time, and then swallows it again. It goes through two more stomachs before it is completely digested. A good milk cow can give as much as 4228 quarts (1057 gallons, or 4000 liters) of milk in a year.

PIG

Male: boar. Castrated: barrow
Female: sow
Young: piglets

After a gestation period of sixteen weeks, the sow "farrows," as the birth of baby pigs is called. Mostly there are ten to twelve piglets. Pigs are "omnivorous"—they will eat both plants and meat. They have long, floppy ears, which are often cocked forward and so cover their tiny eyes. Their good sense of smell helps them find food.

GOAT

Male: buck, ram, billy
Female: doe, ewe, nanny
Young: fawn, kid

The goat is also a ruminant. Goats can live on any kind of fodder and in any climate. They are active and intelligent and very self-willed. The bucks have a little beard we call a "goatee," and in some breeds both buck and doe have one or two little appendages at their throats that are called "the little bell." There are horned and hornless breeds. After a gestation period of twenty-two weeks, the doe bears one or two kids.

SHEEP

Male: buck, ram. Castrated: wether
Female: ewe
Young: lamb

After a gestation period of twenty-two weeks, the ewe bears one or two (or, rarely, three) lambs, which immediately begin to nurse at the two teats on her udder. There are horned and hornless breeds. Like the cow, they are ruminants. They are very obedient and tamely follow the shepherd and his dog, which makes them easy to herd in the fields. Their thick pelts can be shorn twice a year.

CHICKEN

Male: rooster, cock
Female: hen; broody hen (setting hen with chicks)
Young: chicks

The hen lays and broods ten to fourteen eggs, from which the chicks hatch after twenty-two days. Chickens are walking birds and don't fly very well. If they feel threatened, they run away, cackling loudly. Only if there seems to be no other way out will they fly up. If you take away the hen's eggs every day and don't allow her to brood, she will lay 200 to 300 eggs per year. Hens are shy of water and prefer to "bathe" themselves in sand and dust. Their food is corn, for the most part, but they also eat worms and beetles.

DUCK

Male: drake
Female: duck
Young: duckling, chick

In the spring the duck lays and broods ten to fourteen eggs. After four weeks the yolk-yellow ducklings hatch. Ducks have webbed feet and are omnivorous: They eat tadpoles, snails, worms, and plants. A duck needs approximately double the daily amount of food a hen of the same weight does. When the ducklings are big enough, the duck broods a second time.

GOOSE

Male: gander
Female: goose
Young: gosling, chick

In the beginning of April the goose lays and broods twelve to fourteen eggs from which yellow chicks hatch after four weeks. The geese have webbed feet and pull up their plant food with the points of their beaks. Geese have longer necks than ducks do. The gander keeps watch and defends the brooding goose, as he does later with the band of goslings. Goose and gander have the same plumage and are therefore not easy to tell apart.

SWAN

Male: cob
Female: pen
Young: cygnet

Once a year, about the middle of April, the pen

broods her five to eight eggs. Her mate relieves her during this period. After some thirty-five days, the bright-gray young hatch out. As precocial birds, they follow their parents right into the water. Swan pairs mate for life, and they feed their young together.

TURKEY

Male: turkey-cock, tom
Female: turkey-hen
Young: chicks

Once a year the turkey-hen lays eight to fifteen eggs and sets for eighteen days. The turkey chicks leave the nest as soon as their downy coats have dried. They can't endure dampness, so when it rains, they huddle under the wings of the turkey-hen; she literally "takes them under her wing." The turkey can grow to weigh about thirty-three pounds (fifteen kilograms).

Altricial

DOG

Male: dog
Female: bitch
Young: whelps (while nursing); puppies

A bitch can have puppies twice a year. After sixty-three days she bears four to six blind whelps, which open their eyes after about ten days. They are nursed by their mother for about two months. Dogs are "predators," which means they hunt for their food, and therefore they are meat-eaters ("carnivores").

CAT

Male: tomcat
Female: cat
Young: kittens

Generally a cat has anywhere from four to six kittens after a gestation period of eight weeks in spring and in fall. The kittens' eyes are closed for about nine days, and they are not yet able to pull in their claws. Only when they see do they leave the nest. House cats are also predators and therefore are predominantly meat-eaters.

RABBIT

Male: buck
Female: doe
Young: no special name

A doe can have young many times a year. She bears one to nine babies after a gestation period of twenty-eight to thirty-one days. The baby rabbits are born with both their eyes and ears tightly closed. After about ten days their eyes open, and their fur grows. The little ones can hear very early, though.

PIGEON

Male: cock
Female: pigeon, hen
Young: chick

Several times during the year the cock and hen pigeon brood their eggs together for sixteen to eighteen days. They usually have two eggs or, rarely, one or three. When the baby birds hatch, they are helpless. Only after four or five weeks do they grow feathers (a process called "fledging") and can then leave the nest. In their first days, the chicks' nourishment consists of "crop milk," which is produced in the walls of the crop in both parents during the brooding time. Later the chicks pull predigested fruits and seeds out of their parents' crops. A peculiarity of pigeons is that, unlike other birds, they suck up water when drinking.